VINTAGE AMERICAN
FARM TRACTORS

Andrew Morland

Motorbooks International
Publishers & Wholesalers

First published in 1997 by Motorbooks International Publishers & Wholesalers, 729 Prospect Avenue, PO Box 1, Osceola, WI 54020-0001 USA

Library of Congress Cataloging-in-Publication Data

Morland, Andrew.
 Vintage American farm tractors / Andrew Morland.
  p. cm. -- (Enthusiast color series)
 Includes Index.
 ISBN 0-7603-0147-6 (pbk. : alk. paper)
 1. Farm tractors--United States--History. I. Title. II. Series.
 TL233.6.F37M6723   1997
 629.225'2--dc21   97-13562

On the front cover: When it came to big farming chores, nothing could beat this 1955 Minneapolis-Moline Model GB diesel tractor. Weighing nearly 4 tons, this model, produced between 1955 and 1959, was just right for farming large expanses of land.

On the frontispiece: The Cockshutt Model 40, powered by a six-cylinder Buda engine, was introduced in 1949. The last Model 40 rolled off the line in 1957.

On the title page: The Hart-Parr Tractor Company, formed by Charles W. Hart and Charles H. Parr, produced many fine farm tractors. One of them was the 12-24 Model E, which was manufactured between 1924 and 1928.

On the back cover: This 1929 Allis-Chalmers United is equipped with a four-cylinder, flathead Continental engine. Later Model U tractors were powered by an overhead-valve, four-cylinder engine built by Allis-Chalmers.

Printed in Hong Kong through World Print, Ltd.

12 95

Contents

Acknowledgments

Many thanks to all the enthusiastic owners of the tractors photographed for this book. Thanks for their time, hospitality and cooperation, without which completing such a book would be impossible. They are listed below:

John Read
Jay Foxworthy
J.R. Gyger
Jim Grant
Leroy Wonder
Chris Dart
David Preuhs
Dennis Nutt
Rod Flint
Sue Dougan-Twin City Collection
Norm Seveik

Dan Schmitt
Paul Cluyas
Ken Anderson
Peter and Shaun Bennetts
Ivan Sparks
Palmer Fossum
Ralph Oliver
Keller Family
Don Wolf
John Davis
Neal Jackson
Russel Church
Barry Bruce-Scotbury Collection
The Ontario Agricultural Museum, Milton, Canada

Andrew Morland

6

Introduction

The early mechanization of farming began in Scotland, where a reliable working steam plow was built in the 1860s. Early farm tractors were steam traction engines, fueled by coal and wood.

The first farm vehicle successfully powered by a gasoline engine was built by an Iowa blacksmith, John Froehlich, in 1892. The first commercially successful manufacturers, however, were C.W. Hart and C.H. Parr of Charles City, Iowa. Their Number One rolled off the production line in 1901. They were the first company to use the word "tractor" in their advertisements, although the word had been around for years.

The Otto Gas Engine Company built one of the first gasoline tractors, but on a steam traction engine chassis. One of the best designs was built by the Waterloo Gasoline Engine Company. This company was bought in 1918 by John Deere and Company, who used the basis of the Waterloo Boy engine design in John Deere tractors for many years.

The 1920 to 1930 period was the time of tractor mass production. In 1918, Ford manufactured the Fordson F with its cast-iron unit frame. The Fordson was modern and cheap compared to the archaic developments of other companies since 1900. It became incredibly popular, with 104,000 Fordsons built in 1925. In the years between 1930 and 1940, Ford was matched and overtaken by the many successful developments of other tractor manufacturers.

The John Deere General Purpose twin-cylinder tractors sold well. The Model D, introduced in the 1920s, was a compact and powerful tractor that suited the needs of most farmers. The success of the D in the 1930s gave it the distinction of being the largest single-production model ever.

The next decade, from 1940 to 1950, witnessed a significant development that would influence the progress of the tractor. It was the Ferguson three-point hitch system, run by hydraulic power. This system, used on the Ford 9N, 2N, 8N, and Ferguson tractor, would make the farmer's job easier. The Ford N Series was a big success for Ford, with more than 300,000 tractors sold.

It took Ford's competitors quite a few years to succeed with their own versions of Ferguson's three-point hitch. Once they had such a system in the late 1940s and 1950s, manufacturers such as Allis-Chalmers, Case, Cockshutt, John Deere, International, Massey, Minneapolis-Moline, and Oliver experienced considerable worldwide sales. The next decade saw the development of the diesel tractor for economy and reliability.

Today, these tractors may have seen 40 years' work; many are still at work on farms throughout the United States. The quality and strength of a diesel engine can make them expensive to restore, but these 1950s and 1960s vintage diesel tractors are becoming very collectible.

CHAPTER ONE

Allis-Chalmers
TRACTORS

In 1861, Edward P. Allis bought the bankrupt Reliance Works, the biggest iron works in Milwaukee, for $22.72, and renamed it Edward P. Allis and Company. Within four years, annual sales had reached $100,000. When Edward died in 1889, his company merged with a mining equipment company called Frazer and Chalmers, resulting in a name change for the new company to Allis-Chalmers. At the same time, the Gates Iron Works and the Dickson Manufacturing Company, steam boiler producers, joined the merger.

The new company's Steam Division offered an enormous range of Reynolds-Corliss engines, from 100 to 10,000 horsepower.

In 1904, the Bullock Electrical and Manufacturing Company was taken over by A-C so that it could sell a complete package of engines and electrical generators. Unfortunately, the U.S. economy hit a downturn in 1911, and the A-C

The Allis-Chalmers United, built in 1929, with the four-cylinder Continental "SO" side-valve gasoline engine and three-speed gearbox.

9

This Allis-Chalmers United, Serial No. 539, was built in 1929. It was sold by A-C partners, the United Tractor and Equipment Company, with the "United" name cast in the radiator. The A-C dealers sold an identical tractor with "Allis-Chalmers" cast in the radiator.

Company overstretched its finances. By 1912, it went into receivership.

One of the official receivers, General Otto Falk, managed to reorganize the vast A-C Company and set up a new business called the Allis-Chalmers Manufacturing Company. Falk expanded its farm machinery business. The A-C Manufacturing Company took over the Monarch Tractor Corporation in 1928, the Lacrosse Plow Company in 1929, the Stearns Engine Company in 1930, and the Advance-Rumely Thresher Company in 1931.

Allis-Chalmers built their first tractor in the West Allis factory in Wisconsin in 1914. The 10-18 tractor was a three-wheel design, which was popular during this period. The 303-ci horizontally-opposed two-cylinder engine ran on kerosene, but it was started on gasoline. The transmission had only one forward and one reverse gear. The one-piece frame was unusual for the period, as most were multi-riveted. The 10-18 was not a success. Their next tractor, the

An Allis-Chalmers Model B, built in 1938, with steel wheels and special equipment extended fenders and front-end weights around the engine. The Model B was in production from 1937 to 1958.

This Allis-Chalmers 20-30, built in early 1929, was the first model to carry the familiar A-C radiator shape, but in deep-green paint. The famous Persian Orange paint didn't appear until later in 1929.

6-12, was similar to the Moline Universal. A four-cylinder Le Roi Engine Model 20 was rated at 6 drawbar horsepower and 12 PTO horsepower. In four years of production, only 700 were built.

The third A-C tractor was the successful 15-30, which became known as the 18-30 before evolving into the Model E 25-40. The smaller 12-20 was announced in 1921, but after the Nebraska tests, it was reclassified as the 15-25 tractor. In this period, Allis-Chalmers tractors were painted dark green with red or yellow striping.

In 1929, the famous Persian Orange-painted tractors arrived with the A-C Model U.

The U had been developed in only one year, after an order for a new tractor from the United Tractors and Farm Equipment Company, the Chicago-based co-op. Initially, A-C used the P10 Continental four-cylinder 30-horsepower L-head engine. Later, A-C fitted their own 34-horsepower four-cylinder 301-ci overhead-valve engine in the U, renaming the tractor the UM.

The Model U became famous as the first production farm tractor to be offered with low-pressure rubber tires as standard equipment. Allis-Chalmers worked with Firestone on this massive breakthrough in tractor technology. However, the

The Allis-Chalmers 20-30 of 1929 used A-C's own four-cylinder overhead-valve engine, with a 4 3/4 x 6 1/2 inch bore and stroke; it was rated at 20-35 horsepower.

WC launched in 1933 was a much better seller than the Model U. The A-C smooth high-revving four-cylinder 201-ci lightweight engine powered the WC. The two-plow tractor was a great success, with more than 178,000 built before production finished in 1948.

In 1936, the big and powerful Model A was launched to replace the aging Model E. The standard-tread Model A weighed 7,120 pounds with its four-cylinder 461-ci engine. Production finished in 1941 after only 1,200 were built.

The Model B, launched in 1937, sold incredibly well worldwide. The lightweight B cost less than $500, which helped sales reach 120,000 before production finished at the West Allis plant in 1957. The four-cylinder A-C 116-ci was powerful enough for most farmers, but in 1943, the engine was enlarged to 125-ci capacity. In 1958, the British A-C factory in Lincolnshire uprated the B and designated it as the D270. This model used the A-C four-cylinder gasoline engine, or the three-cylinder P3 Perkins diesel engine. In 1959, the British factory developed the D272, with a more-powerful 30-horsepower gasoline engine and better hydraulics. In 1960, a completely new tractor, the ED40, was manufactured by the British factory. Unfortunately, this tractor was underdeveloped: the 138-ci Standard-Ricardo diesel engine had many design faults that caused the ED40 to break down often, and it would not start in cold weather. Sales were very disappointing on both sides of the Atlantic.

In the United States, Allis-Chalmers brought out the unpopular RC in 1939. It was designed to fit between the Models B and WC in the tractor range. The RC used the B's four-cylinder 125-ci engine, making it underpowered and overweight. Only 5,500 were sold. The upgraded B, called the Model C, was introduced in 1940 to replace the RC. Weighing 800 pounds less than the RC, it became a popular tractor.

The radical Model G tractor, constructed for front-mounted implements used to cultivate vegetables in market gardens and small holdings, was announced in 1948. The Continental four-cylinder 10.3-belt-horsepower-engined G was manufactured at Gadsen in Alabama, and at Dieppe in France. A-C had a good share of the limited market for such small tractors, but fewer than 30,000 were built between 1948 and 1955.

The replacement for the WC, the WD, was launched in 1948. The WD used the more-powerful 226-ci "Power Crater" engine, while the WD45 diesel tractor used the 43.3-belt-horsepower six-cylinder Buda diesel of 230-ci capacity. The WDs came with "Two-Clutch Power Control," power-shift wheels and "Traction Booster." In 1957, production of the WD45 ended with an impressive total of 90,000 having been built.

The first of the D Series tractors was launched in 1958 with the three-plow D14 and the four/five-plow D17 tractors. The D Series

An Allis-Chalmers WD45 diesel. The six-cylinder Buda 6BD-230 diesel engine has a 3.438-inch bore and 4.125-inch stroke, giving a displacement of 230 ci.

The Allis-Chalmers D272, built at the English Essendine factory, has the three-cylinder Perkins P3 144-ci engine developing 31 horsepower at 1,900 rpm.

would eventually replace the whole Allis-Chalmers range of tractors. The D14 used the 149-ci four-cylinder engine derived from the WD. The D17 used the A-C 226-ci engine with higher compression, producing 52.7 belt horsepower. The diesel used the 262-ci six-cylinder engine.

The A-C D19 tractor gave the company another first in the history of tractor development. In 1961, the D19 was the first turbocharged diesel-powered tractor. Diesel trucks had used turbo-charged engines since the mid-1950s, but its use in a tractor was revolutionary. It gave the D19 more power without the extra weight of a larger engine. The six-cylinder 262-ci Garrett turbo diesel A-C engine tractor was rated at 66.92 belt horsepower and 61.27 drawbar horsepower.

The Allis-Chalmers ED40 was manufactured in the A-C factory at Essendine, Lincolnshire, England, from 1960 to 1968. It was powered by the Standard-Ricardo 137.9-ci diesel engine.

The Allis-Chalmers Model M crawler was a development on the Monarch crawler. Allis-Chalmers had acquired the Monarch Tractor Corporation in 1928. A total of 14,524 of the M were produced from 1932 to 1942.

In 1963, the all-new D21 was produced with a new transmission and a 426-ci diesel engine rated at 103 PTO horsepower. In 1965, the D21 was turbo-charged to give 128 PTO horsepower. The new squared styling of the D21 was carried over into the hundred series in 1969.

The One-Ninety was the first new model in the hundred series, followed by the 175, 180, 185, 190, and the 190 XT. The XT was the turbo-charged version of the 190, producing 93.6 PTO horsepower and was also the best selling of the 100 Series.

In the late 1970s, the 1,000 Series was born. The Model 6070 was the last tractor made by the Allis-Chalmers assembly line on December 6, 1985. However, despite Deutz buying the A-C Company and closing down the tractor production at the West Allis plant, a management buyout of the company a year later revived the A-C name. The new company, AGCO, produced a range of tractors from 40 to 215 horsepower, using the AGCO-ALLIS name. Today, the AGCO Corporation is the biggest manufacturer of tractors in the world.

The Allis-Chalmers ED40 Depthomatic, built at Essendine in 1966, with the Standard-Ricardo 23C diesel engine producing 41 brake horsepower from 137.9-ci displacement.

CHAPTER TWO

Case
TRACTORS

Jerome Increase Case founded the J.I. Case Threshing Machine Company in Rochester, Wisconsin, in 1842. The company's first product was the groundhog-type threshing machine. After only two years of production, Case moved his manufacturing business to Racine, Wisconsin, because of problems over water rights at Rochester.

In 1865, the Civil War bald eagle mascot "Old Abe," named after President Lincoln, became the Case trademark.

Jerome Case started a second company at Racine in 1876. Called the J.I. Case Plow Works, it was created to build plows. It was eventually controlled by the Wallis Tractor Company, which sold out to Massey-Harris in 1920. In 1928, Massey sold the rights of the Case name back to the J.I. Case Threshing Machine Company.

The first Case internal-combustion-engined tractor was built in 1892. One of the world's earliest

The Case DO, built in 1950, with full fenders, branch deflectors, and cowling for use in orchards. Only 2,874 were manufactured from 1939 to 1952. Total D Series production was over 100,000, despite the 15-month strike that started in December 1945.

The 1950 Case DO had the same mechanical specification as the standard Model D. At the Nebraska Tests of 1940, the four-cylinder engine with 3 7/8 x 5 1/2 bore and stroke produced 32 belt horsepower.

A Case 200 Series, built in 1958, with the 12-speed "Tripl-Range" transmission. It is powered by the four-cylinder 126.5-ci Case engine.

tractors was built, unfortunately, before the knowledge of the workings of carburetors and ignition designs was known. Because of this, the Case-Paterson two-cylinder four-stroke spark-ignition engine tractor was not put into production.

The J.I. Case Threshing Machine Company returned to steam traction engine manufacturing until 1911, when they brought out the massive two-cylinder 12-ton 30-60 horsepower model. The small 20-40 horsepower soon followed, then the 12-25 horsepower, and lastly the 10-20 horsepower in 1915.

The famous crossmotor Cases evolved from the 10-20 horsepower into the 9-18 horsepower of 1916. In 1918, Case introduced the 9-18 B, built on a one-piece cast-iron frame. This modern design made for a structurally strong but lightweight tractor.

The crossmotor Case tractors sold well and the range expanded to include the 15-27, 18-32, 22-40, 25-45, and 40-72 horsepower models. The overhead-valve four-cylinder engines were started on gasoline and, when warm, could be switched onto kerosene. In 1928, more than 50,000 of the 12-20, 18-32, and 25-45 horsepower crossmotor tractors had been sold around the world.

The Case Model VC of 1941 has a Continental L-head four-cylinder engine that is rated at 22.07 belt horsepower and 15.07 drawbar horsepower. The transmission and gears were produced by the Clark Company.

In 1929, the new line of tractors was launched with the Model L. It was a conventional unitized tractor with a longitudinal four-cylinder engine rated at 40 belt PTO horsepower and 26 drawbar horsepower. Later, in 1929, the smaller Model C tractor became available. It was rated as a 17-27 horsepower tractor capable of pulling two to three 14-inch plows.

In 1935, the Model CC came out with "Motor Lift." This mechanically driven implement lift worked through a clutch for attaching implements. Also in 1935, the little RC range was introduced, using the 11-to-17-horsepower Waukesha four-cylinder engine; it was rated as a two-plow tractor.

There was a major change to the whole range of Case tractors in 1939. The tractors were restyled and the color was changed from gray to the bright Flambeau Red. This modernization from angular styling to curved radiators, and the change of color, turned the Flambeau series of Case tractors into the company's best-selling range ever. The J.I. Case Company became number three in the tractor market, behind International and John Deere.

Between 1939 and 1955, the Flambeau series included the D, LA, S, V, and VA models. In this period, Case produced slightly fewer than 390,000 tractors.

In 1953, the first of the next series of Case tractors was launched with the Model 500. This was an uprated and improved Model LA that had an option of gasoline, LPG, or diesel engines. With the new series came a change of color, with Desert Sand for all the sheet metal, and the old Flambeau Red for

The Case LA standard of 1951 had a 403-ci four-cylinder Case engine that produced 52.5 belt horsepower at 1,100 rpm.

the rest of the tractor. The 500 Case was followed by the 400 mid-range, and the large 600 in 1955, then the small 300 row-crop tractor in 1956.

In 1967, Tenneco Inc. became the biggest shareholder in Case, and the Tenneco chairman, Nelson Freeman, became the chairman of Case. By 1972, the new company was booming, with profits of $610 million. That year, it bought the David Brown Tractor Company in Britain. Case then produced the smaller Case tractors in the David Brown factory for the U.S. market.

The Case 400 orchard of 1955 was the replacement for the Model D tractor. It was one of the first Case tractors to be fitted with a foot-operated clutch.

In 1984, Tenneco bought part of the International Harvester Company, and the tractor color scheme changed to International Red with a Case black-and-silver stripe. The Case and International Harvester emblems were joined together.

The Case 400 orchard was offered with either a 49.4-horsepower diesel unit or a 53.25-horsepower gasoline engine. Both powerplants were four-cylinder Case engines of 25.1-ci.

This view of the 1955 Case 400 orchard shows the comfortable cushioned seat, which is sprung by torsion rubber and is tiltable. Note that the branch protector cowling over the steering has holes for ventilation.

The Case 400 high-crop is also known as the high-clearance sugar cane special. It is very rare and collectible.

The 400 Series was built from 1955 to 1960. The Case 251-ci engines were available in diesel, gasoline, or LPG configurations.

CHAPTER THREE

Ferguson
TRACTORS

Harry Ferguson was born in 1884 in County Down, in the north of Ireland. He was one of 11 children living on the family's 100-acre farm. When he was old enough, he worked with horses on the farm. In 1902, he went to Belfast to work with his elder brother, Joe, in his bicycle and motorcycle workshop. He successfully raced motorcycles that he had prepared, and the winning of races brought more business to the Ferguson brothers. They must have been prosperous, because in 1908, he showed off his mechanical skills by building his own aircraft. In 1909, he became the first person in Britain to design and fly his own aircraft, and recorded the first flight in Ireland. After building three more aircraft, and crashing a few times, he decided it was time to start his own business.

He opened an agency for the Waterloo Boy tractor, known as the "Overtime" in Belfast. This tractor, manufactured by the Waterloo

The Ferguson TEA-20 was built at the Banner Lane Standard Motor Company factory in Coventry, England. TE versions were built in England and TO versions were built in the United States.

29

A Ferguson TEA-20 built in Great Britain in 1949. Owned by the Ferguson factory, it was used at agricultural shows to sell their tractors.

Gasoline Engine Company of Waterloo, Iowa, was taken over by John Deere in 1918.

It was a good period in which to have a tractor dealership in Britain. During World War I, the German U-boats had prevented food from reaching Britain. To improve food production, farm tractors were needed in great numbers. While selling and demonstrating plowing with the Overtime, he imagined improvements in the plow. Ferguson's first patent, for the Belfast plow, came out in September 1917. He designed and fitted many plows to the Eros tractor, a lightweight Ford Model T conversion kit produced by the Staude Company of St. Paul, Minnesota.

These conversions sold well until Ford brought out the F Model Fordson. However, Ferguson's new Duplex hitch, which helped to keep the plow in the ground, sold well to F owners because it stopped these tractors from turning over. When the standard plow hit obstructions, the whole tractor pulled itself over backwards, crushing the driver. The Fordson had killed 136 farmers in the United States in 1922.

The 1949 Ferguson TE-20 engine is a development of the 2-liter Standard-Vanguard gasoline car engine, which replaced the Continental engine in Great Britain in 1948. The U.S. market used the overhead-valve Continental 24-horsepower 1,966-cc engine.

Neal Jackson plows at the Great Dorset Team Fair with his immaculately restored Massey-Ferguson 35 Deluxe.

Ferguson spent many years working on his concept of a single tractor/implement unit, and it was finally demonstrated to the public in 1933. David Brown was impressed with the Ferguson prototype tractor and went into partnership with Ferguson. In 1936, production started at the David Brown factory near Huddersfield, Yorkshire. There was much public and press interest, but sales were slow. Only 1,350 were built before production finished in 1939. The main problem with the Ferguson-Brown tractor was the price at £224, while a Fordson Model N cost only £140.

Harry Ferguson's next move had a dramatic effect on tractor history. He took the Ferguson tractor to Henry Ford's Fair Lane Estate at Dearborn to demonstrate the Ferguson system. The meeting ended with the famous handshake agreement, which was not witnessed or recorded. Ford agreed to put the tractor into volume production, and Ferguson would market the tractor and implements.

On June 29, 1939, the Ford 9N, with the Ferguson System in Ferguson gray colors, was shown to the public. Sales of Ford N Series tractors totaled

The 1958 Massey-Ferguson 35 Deluxe tractor, built in Coventry, England, was the development of the Ferguson 35, which was painted gray and gold. The same tractor was marketed in North America as the Massey-Harris 50, using the Continental 2134 engine of 133.6 ci.

300,000 up to 1952. Ferguson had hoped that sales would be higher as the British Ford plant at Dagenham would produce the 8N after the war. This never happened, and the breakup with Ford began.

When Henry Ford II took over Ford, the situation got worse. Ford was losing money on the 9N, and they wished to have control over marketing and bringing out new models. Ferguson had a large distribution company in the United States and would have no tractors to sell. On a visit to

Dearborn, Ferguson was appalled to see the latest 8N with all his patented systems, and without any new agreement. He immediately started legal action against Ford. At the same time, he quickly established a new Ferguson factory in Detroit. In Britain, he managed to get the Standard Motor Company to produce the TE Ferguson in their Banner Lane factory, located in Coventry, by 1946. The American-built Ferguson was called the TO20, based on the British TE20. Before the

Neal Jackson's Massey-Ferguson 35 Deluxe. A Marshall tractor can be seen in the background.

American factory was up and running, 25,000 TE20s were shipped to the United States. Ferguson won a claim against Ford and received $9.25 million. In addition, Ford had to change the three-point-hitch system to their own design.

The Ferguson TE20 was a great improvement over the 9N, with a more-powerful engine and an extra forward gear. At the Banner Lane factory in Coventry, 517,651 Ferguson TE20 tractors were manufactured between 1946 and 1956.

Harry Ferguson, like Henry Ford, had an economic philosophy to fight inflation by price reduction. However, this reduced the Ferguson Company profits. He was eventually forced to sell the Detroit factory to Massey-Harris, and later the whole company, due to his poor health. In August 1953, he received $16 million worth of Massey-

Harris shares, and a position of chairman and controller of tractor design. The new company was called Massey-Harris-Ferguson, and later changed to Massey-Harris. It wasn't long before Ferguson resigned, due to lack of progress in putting the Ferguson TE60 into production.

The first new Ferguson TO35s, from the Massey-Ferguson Company, were painted gray and gold. This tractor used the Z134 Continental engine of 133.61-ci, with a six-speed transmission. In 1957, the TO35 was painted in the new Massey-Ferguson red colors, and the name had changed to MF35. The MF35, MF25, and the French-built MF825 were outstanding successes.

Harry Ferguson died in 1960, leaving behind a massive contribution to the modernization of farming.

The business end of a rare four-wheel-drive Ferguson T20 shows the Ferguson System three-point hitch. These T20 tractors were converted to four-wheel drive by Selene of Turin, Italy.

CHAPTER FOUR

Ford
TRACTORS

Henry Ford was born in 1863 on the family farm in Dearborn, Wayne County, Michigan. He did not enjoy life on the farm, and even said "it was just too much work." As soon as he possibly could, he left for work in Detroit.

After the failure of his first two business ventures, the Detroit Automobile Company and the Henry Ford Company, he founded the Ford Motor Company in 1903. The Ford Model T car was a triumph of mass production, ensuring incredibly low manufacturing costs, and a low purchase price. Henry Ford wished to produce a modern tractor by the same method, thus keeping costs down. He experimented with a tractor based on the Ford car chassis. The first successful prototype tractor—the "Automobile Plow," based on a Model B car engine—appeared in 1907.

In 1916, a Ford engineer named Eugene Farkas designed a four-wheel four-cylinder three-speed frameless tractor. The engine, transmission,

A 1936 Fordson N, serial number 807343, is fitted with a power take-off Plymouth Gear Shift pulley. It has a standard water washer air cleaner but a non-standard short exhaust pipe.

This 1938 Fordson standard Model N was built in Dagenham, England. It is seen here at the European Plowing Championships in Wellington, England.

and differential were all part of the chassis, similar to the Wallis Cub tractor. Fifteen prototypes were built using the 251-ci Hercules engine. The British, engaged in World War I, were worried about food production. The Ministry of Munitions ordered 6,000 tractors from Ford, hoping that they would be produced at Dagenham in Britain. Due to production problems, the new tractor was manufactured in Dearborn. Henry Ford set up a company with his son, Edsel, and named the new company Fordson.

The new tractor, called the Model F, went into production in 1917, but only 259 were built. By 1918, 34,000 were made with a similar specifi-

cation to the prototype, but with a Ford-built 251-ci four-cylinder L-head engine and three-speed gearbox. The engine was rated at 10 drawbar horsepower and 20 belt horsepower. The advanced modern design and low price helped sales worldwide. The peak production year was 1925, with 104,168 tractors built. Production finished in 1928 in the United States, after 739,977 tractors had been built. By 1928, the F was losing sales to more modern tractors, and Ford wished to use the factory space for the Ford Model A car.

The replacement for the F was the Model N tractor in 1929. The production started in Cork,

This 1954 Fordson Major has a type 64 conversion by Stormont Engineering of Kent, England. This model was designed for use in sawmills or forestry work.

Ireland. The major change was that the engine had been enlarged to a more-powerful 267-ci capacity, with magneto ignition. In 1932, Ford moved the production from Cork to Dagenham in England. The English Model N production started in February 1933. This gave Ford time to give the Model N a face lift. The color was changed from gray to dark blue, and the Fordson name appeared in the side of the radiator castings, which were now ribbed.

In 1937, the Dagenham factory produced 18,698 tractors, but the Fordson design was 20 years old. To improve sales, the Fordson All-Round row crop was introduced the same year. In 1937, the oil bath air cleaner replaced the water washer filter system. The 1938 model was painted bright orange, but was changed to green the next year— World War II had started and the orange Fordsons were an obvious target for the Luftwaffe.

In 1945, the Dagenham plant brought out the postwar development of the Model N, the E27N Major. The big change for the latest Fordson was the adoption of a conventional differential from the Model N's power-absorbing and expensive old worm and worm wheel final drive. The four-cylinder mixed-fuel tractor was rated at

This Fordson Major E27N was built in 1946. This model uses the four-cylinder L-head Model N engine, uprated to 30 horsepower at 1,450 rpm. The N-model engine had been designed back in 1917.

The 1954 Fordson Major is powered by Ford's own 3.6-liter four-cylinder diesel engine.

The 30-horsepower four-cylinder N engine proved powerful enough because Ford at last used a spiral-bevel differential, which replaced their normal power-sapping worm drive.

28.5 belt horsepower and 19.1 drawbar horsepower. The E27N was manufactured for seven years with gasoline/TVO and diesel engines. The Perkins six-cylinder diesel engine of 289 ci and 45 horsepower was offered from 1948.

Ford N Series

Harry Ferguson had produced a three-point hydraulic hitch for his first tractor, the Ferguson-Brown, in England. Ferguson brought his Ferguson-Brown tractor and plow to Ford's Fair Lane Estate and demonstrated it to Henry Ford. The Ferguson tractor completely outplowed the Fordson and the other tractors in a test. After the demonstration, Henry Ford shook hands with Ferguson in a historic agreement. Ford would manufacture the tractor, while Ferguson would be in charge of marketing and design. The tractor was called the 9N and it was an immediate success when it was launched in June 1939. A total of 10,000 were sold before 1940.

The 9N used a 119.5-ci four-cylinder engine. The success of the Ford 9N tractor was due in equal part to Ford's mass-production methods and to the Ferguson integral three-point hitch system. The Ferguson internal hydraulic system raised or lowered the implements via two lower links. The upper link connected to the hydraulic control

The Major E27N seems much larger than the earlier Model N Fordson, but the main difference is the use of large-diameter wheels on the Major. This tractor was a great success for Ford, with more than 50,000 manufactured at the peak of production in 1948 at Dagenham.

valve, with coil springs controlling the depth of the plow. In 1942, the 9N became the 2N.

The postwar 8N caused the breakup of the Ford-Ferguson partnership. Ford wished to market their own tractors through Dearborn Motors. Ferguson was left with no tractors to sell through his marketing company, and started his own Ferguson Tractor Company in Britain, and later in the United States.

Ferguson sued Ford for $251 million for patent infringement and loss of business. In 1952, Ferguson won only $9.25 million, but Ford was forced to change the Ferguson three-point hydraulic system.

In 1952, Ford redesigned the hydraulic hitch and upgraded the complete tractor. The result was the production of the NAA Jubilee Model in 1953, the 50th anniversary of the Ford Motor Company. The restyled Golden Jubilee Model was fitted with a new overhead-valve four-cylinder 134-ci engine. In 1955, the 100 Series, based on the Jubilee, was launched. The 600 Model used the 134-ci engine, and was followed by the 800, with a new 172-ci overhead-valve engine. The range expanded to include the 500, 700, and 900, before the 1,000 Series appeared in 1961.

A Ford 8N-C, built in late 1952, the last year of production. The 8N was manufactured from 1947 to 1952 with 524,076 built.

The four-cylinder 119.7-ci engine of the 1952 Ford Model 8N-C used a higher compression ratio than the earlier 9N model, producing more power. A four-speed transmission was standard; the previous models had only three gears.

The Ford 8N-C with a Ford Dearborn Model 10-1 two-bottom 14-inch plow. The Dearborn Motors Ford subsidiary offered more than 400 implements for the 8N tractor.

CHAPTER FIVE

International-
Harvester
TRACTORS

The McCormick Harvesting Machine Company, based in Chicago, had grown to be the largest reaper company in the United States by 1890. The mechanization of farming had also created another large harvesting equipment company in Chicago, the William Deering Company, which was expanding fast with many new patented inventions, such as the "Marsh" harvester.

In 1902, the Deering Company merged with the McCormick Harvesting Machine Company to become the International Harvester Company. The name was chosen by George Perkins, a partner of McCormick. At the same time, the new company acquired the Plano Manufacturing Company, the Warder, Bushnell and Glessner Company, and the Milwaukee Harvester Company. Now with 85 percent of the U.S. harvester production under one company, large profits seemed guaranteed. These profits were used to finance the first International tractor.

An International-McCormick Farmall FB HV high-crop tractor built in 1948.

The high-crop version of the Model H uses the 152-ci four-cylinder engine that produces 25 horsepower. Roller chain final drive is used to raise the rear axle.

The International Harvester Company owned iron works, coal and iron mines, and the Illinois Northern Railway. One of the companies acquired was the Milwaukee Company, which made stationary engines. Another company in Upper Sandusky, Ohio, built trucks. In 1906, the first International tractor was built at Upper Sandusky, using the engines shipped down from the Milwaukee Company.

The first tractor was a 15-horsepower model, using a single-cylinder four-stroke open-crank engine. This was followed in 1908 by the 20-horsepower and 40-horsepower tractors manufactured at the Milwaukee factory.

In 1911, the Mogul 45-horsepower two-cylinder horizontally-opposed engine tractor was launched. This was followed by the smaller and more-popular 10-20 Titan of 1914. This also used a horizontally-opposed two-cylinder engine, rated at 20 horsepower at 575 rpm. This engine was cooled by a large cylindrical water tank mounted on the chassis at the front of the tractor.

Production of the modern-looking 8-16, known in Britain as the International Junior, began in 1917. This tractor used the four-cylinder engine, hood, and radiator from the International truck.

Many years had been spent fighting the U.S. government's antitrust laws. In 1918, the I.H.

A 1936 McCormick-Deering W-12. Only 4,000 standard-tread W-12s were manufactured. They are very collectible today.

Company lost its fight with the government and had to sell some factories and dealerships. The same year, mass production of the Fordson F started, which was soon seen by International Harvester as a threat to their future. I.H. fought back in 1921 with a new range of chassis-less modern tractors, beginning with the 15-30 tractor with the new four-cylinder overhead-valve 382-ci engine. Then the 10-20, with a similar design of engine but with 284-ci capacity, came out in 1923.

The company needed a completely new range of tractors to fight Fordson sales. Alexander Legge was made general manager and given responsibility for organizing the Experimental Department,

The International-McCormick Farmall AV high-crop was designed for use with asparagus and sugar cane. This model has six more inches of ground clearance than the standard A. This is achieved by using longer front kingpin extensions and larger rear tires of 36 x 8 inches.

The International-McCormick Farmall Model B is very similar to the Model A, but with a single or narrow dual front wheel in typical row-crop tractor tradition.

which was run by Edward Johnston, to develop a new tractor. The talented engineers produced the first prototype in 1922, and, in 1924, 200 preproduction models were tested by farmers. A few modifications were made, and the new model went into production. Management was worried about resistance to such a revolutionary idea as an all-purpose row-crop tractor. There was no press launch or major advertising, and the new tractor named Farmall was only sold in Texas at first.

The Farmall was a massive success and other manufacturers were quickly forced to produce their own all-purpose tractors. International Harvester kept an unchallenged top position in tractor sales from 1926 to 1939, when Ford fought back with the Ford-Ferguson 9N. Sales of the

51

The International-McCormick Farmall B cultivation row-crop model. The operator's seat is offset, but unlike the Model A, the rear axle is set in the center with equal axle length on each side.

Farmall could have been even higher if I.H. had invested in "Ford-style" full mass production to get costs down.

The Farmall range started with the tractor we now call the Regular. When tested on kerosene at Nebraska, it produced 12.7 drawbar horsepower and 20.1 belt horsepower from the four-cylinder 221-ci engine.

The Regular was replaced by the F20 and F30 in 1932. The F12 was offered in the same year, but the F14 was only available in 1938 and 1939. The standard-tread tractor models were given the W letter instead of F.

In the late 1930s, I.H. employed industrial designer Raymond Loewy to restyle the International tractors and other products. The new Lettered Series of tractors was launched in 1939, with modern rounded-smooth metal panels, and a new bright-red color. The Model H Farmall was the first to appear, with a new 152-ci four-cylinder engine and a five-speed gearbox. This was followed by the W4 and W6 tractor in 1940. The W denotes a standard-tread tractor. The Model A and B tractors were produced from 1939, with the 113.1-ci four-cylinder 16.8-belt-horsepower engine. The M came out at the same time with the four-cylinder 36-belt-horsepower 247.7-ci engine.

The Super Series identified the change to built-in hydraulics called "Touch Control," which appeared first with the Super A in 1947. This was

RIGHT: The International-McCormick Farmall A uses the four-cylinder 113.1-ci engine that was used in the F-12 and F-14. It is rated at 16.8 belt/PTO horsepower on gasoline and 16.5 belt/PTO horsepower on distillate.

Kenneth Anderson on his nicely restored International-McCormick Farmall B, which was built in 1946. When Nebraska-tested in 1939, the Model B, using gasoline, produced 16.8 horsepower on the belt and 12.1 horsepower at the drawbar.

A 1947 International-McCormick Farmall Cub with owner Kenneth Anderson at the controls. The Cub uses a four-cylinder L-head 10-horsepower 59.5-ci engine.

followed by the Super C in 1951, the Super H, M, and the W6 Standard in 1952.

The Farmall new 100 Series was built from 1954 to 1958. The first International tractor to be shown to the public using this numerical designation was the 123-ci Farmall 200 gasoline tractor, which replaced the Super C. In 1958, the 100 Series was restyled with a more-aggressive-looking radiator grill to keep the tractors up to date. The 460 and 560 Farmall launched that year came with a choice of gasoline, LPG, or diesel engines. The 460 used the 221-ci gasoline or LPG six-cylinder engine. The diesel model had the new six-cylinder International Harvester diesel engine of 236 ci. The 560 used a larger 263-ci six-cylinder for the gasoline or LPG model. The 281-ci International Harvester engine was used in the diesel model.

The 1970s and 1980s were a difficult and tough period for U.S. tractor producers. International Harvester was short of financial capital, and in 1988, Tenneco bought the Tractor and Implement Divisions of International Harvester.

This view of the 0-12 shows the sweeping fenders and exhaust pipe routed under the frame to the rear. The four-cylinder 113-ci gasoline engine was rated at 16.2 belt/PTO horsepower.

A 1937 McCormick-Deering 0-12. This is the orchard version of the F-12/W-12, with sweeping fenders to reduce damage to fruit trees.

CHAPTER SIX

John Deere
TRACTORS

John Deere started his own blacksmith business at Grand Detour, Illinois, in 1836, specializing in his now-famous steel plows. The plow was so popular that in order to expand the business, he moved the J.D. Plow Works in 1848 to Moline, on the Mississippi, so that coal and steel could be shipped in by barge.

The John Deere Company expanded the plant and products to include many different farm implements, harvesters, wagons, bicycles, and buggies. The John Deere Company wished to get into the tractor business and had studied the progress of various companies. John Froelich in Iowa had built and sold two tractors in 1892. However, these were not a great success, as the owners were so dissatisfied they returned the tractors.

Twenty years later, Froelich's company, the Waterloo Gasoline Engine Company of Waterloo, Iowa, introduced the Waterloo Boy tractor. This tractor was a great success. It was developed from

A John Deere Model BR. This rare tractor is similar to the BO and uses the 149-ci two-cylinder engine, which produces 14.3 belt horsepower. In 1938, the power was increased to 17.5 belt horsepower with the 175-ci two-cylinder engine.

A 1929 John Deere GP. This rare side-steer tricycle tractor has chain final drive. Only 23 GP tricycles were built between 1928 and 1929. The 312-ci two-cylinder engine produced 10 horsepower at the drawbar and 20 horsepower at the PTO belt.

The Waterloo Boy Model N, built in 1920, has the horizontal two-cylinder 465-ci engine, producing 25 belt horsepower at 750 rpm. The N has a two-speed transmission, unlike earlier models, which had only one speed.

the Model R in 1914 to the Model N Kerosene in 1917, which was rated at 12 drawbar horsepower and 25 belt horsepower, with a two-forward-speed transmission. More than 8,000 Waterloo Boy tractors had been sold before 1918, when the John Deere Company bought and renamed the company as the John Deere Tractor Company.

The mass-produced Fordson F was selling in vast numbers and taking sales away from all the U.S. tractor manufacturers. The John Deere engineers worked quickly in the tractor development department. They decided to continue with the two-cylinder type engines, as used in the Waterloo Boy. The engine was simple: it had four moving parts that could be made larger and stronger than a multi-cylinder engine, plus the bonus of more low-end torque. The two-cylinder engine had a low build cost and low operating costs, and it was simple for the farmer to repair and service.

The new Model D tractor rolled off the assembly line in late 1923, the first Waterloo Boy tractor to bear the John Deere name. The engine was compact and an integral part of the chassis, like the Fordson and Wallis tractors. The Model D was an enormous success from the launch and,

A 1935 John Deere Model D. This was the first year for the three-speed D. The 5,270-pound tractor is powered by a 501-ci two-cylinder engine, which produces 42 belt horsepower and 30 horsepower at the drawbar.

with updates in design and specifications, stayed in production for 30 years.

The D standard-tread tractor was big and rugged, but it was not capable of doing all the jobs on the farm, such as planting and cultivating. The International Harvester Farmall row-crop tractor was taking sales away from John Deere. So in 1928, John Deere brought out the Model GP (general purpose) tractor. It was the first tractor to integrate a power-lift for its implements. The GP was still a standard-tread tractor, so John Deere quickly brought out GPWT (wide tread) and tricycle GP tractors. Later, the row-crop Models A, B, and G, with adjustable treads and hydraulic lifts, were offered. Many new variations and types were built, including industrial, crawler, and orchard models.

These Deere tractors remained unstyled until the company employed the New York designer Henry Dreyfuss to restyle the range. The first two models to be restyled were the A and B in 1939.

This 1935 John Deere Model D is fitted with 8-28 rubber rear tires and 7.50-18 front tires. Total production from 1923 to 1953 was approximately 160,000.

These new models were well received by the farmers, and the rest of the range were restyled. However, the AR and AO were not given the new look until 1949.

The two-digit series was announced in 1953, with the Model 40 followed by the 50, 60, and 70. The 70 J.D. diesel was the first J.D. row-crop diesel. The two-cylinder diesel engine was started by engaging the V-4 gasoline pony motor. On later models, the pony engine was dropped in favor of a bigger, more powerful, battery.

The three-digit series of tractors was still powered by the two-cylinder engines, with an option of gasoline, tractor fuel, LPG, or diesel in the Models 720 and 730. The 430 used the GM two-cylinder two-stroke supercharged diesel engine, but was the last two-cylinder to be added to the John Deere line in late 1958.

The new generation of John Deere tractors arrived at the end of the 1960 model year. The new line of farm and industrial tractors had been

This 1930 Model GP weighs 3,600 pounds and has the 339-ci engine, which has a bore and stroke of 6 inches. The transmission has three forward gears and one reverse.

A John Deere GPWT, built in 1933, with "over-the-top" steering. It is powered by the 339-ci two-cylinder engine, giving 26.2 drawbar horsepower and 29.6 PTO/belt horsepower.

secretly developed over the previous seven years. The new series was brought out to satisfy the demand for more power and modern multi-cylinder engines.

The new John Deere 1010, 2010, and 3010 tractors were fitted with J.D. gasoline and diesel four-cylinder engines. The 4010 used the six-cylinder gasoline, LPG, and diesel John Deere engines.

With the new series of John Deere tractors, the company began to quickly expand its global business. The company already had manufacturing plants in Argentina and Mexico, and in 1956, it acquired the German Lanz tractor company. Later, it was producing tractors in France, Spain, South Africa, and Australia.

Today, John Deere and Company has grown from a small one-man blacksmith workshop in Grand Detour to a great international company, selling the largest number of one-make tractors in the United States.

A 1959 John Deere Model 430W gasoline row-crop utility tractor. Its 113.5-ci engine was rated at 27.08 drawbar horsepower and 29.21 belt horsepower. The 430 was produced from 1958 to 1961. LPG- and distillate-fueled 113.5-ci engines were offered.

The John Deere Model GP of 1930 has the 339-ci two-cylinder engine, which produces 16 drawbar horsepower and 24 PTO/belt horsepower.

This 1960 Model 435 has the GM two-cycle two-cylinder supercharged diesel engine of 106.1 ci. Only 4,488 were produced. At the Nebraska tests, it was rated at 32.9 horsepower at the belt and 28.4 horsepower at the drawbar.

The styled Model D, produced from 1939 to 1953, has the 501-ci two-cylinder engine.

CHAPTER SEVEN

Minneapolis-Moline
TRACTORS

Using the Twin City name, the Minneapolis Steel and Machinery Company of Minneapolis, Minnesota, had been producing heavyweight tractors since 1902. In 1912, they were contracted by J.I. Case Threshing Machine Company to build 500 Case 30-60 tractors. In 1913, they had an even bigger order from the Bull Company of Minneapolis to manufacture 4,600 tractors, using the Bull engine. The M.S.M. Company wanted to build their own smaller tractor. The Twin City 60-, 40-, 25-, and 15-horsepower tractors were overweight, expensive to produce, and looked like steam traction engines. Sales were declining fast. Most of the sales were to county road departments, not to farmers.

The M.S.M. Company got major government contracts between 1915 and 1918 to manufacture shells for World War I. With the profits from these contracts, the company had enough

The Minneapolis-Moline GB diesel six-cylinder engine has a bore of 4 1/4 inches and a stroke of 5 inches. The cylinder block and head components were the same as the UB four-cylinder diesel. The GB-D was manufactured from 1955 to 1959.

69

This Twin City 16-30 of 1918 was the first of the conventional low-line tractors from the Minneapolis Steel and Machinery Company.

capital to produce their new smaller tractor in 1918. This Twin City tractor, the 16-30, was a modern-looking low-line tractor, but still with separate girder chassis rails. It was built for one year, and only 702 were produced. The four-cylinder Twin City-built engine was bedeviled by starting problems, and gained a terrible reputation.

In 1919, a much-superior Twin City tractor was announced to the public. This was the 12-20, with its revolutionary engine design, which gave 17 drawbar and 28 belt horsepower. The four-cylinder engine had 16 valves, a first for a tractor. Many tractors of the period, and up to the late 1940s, were still using side-valve engines. The use of two intake and two exhaust valves permitted greater intake of fuel and quicker exhaust exit.

After 1919, the M.S.M. tractor range slowly expanded with the 20-35, 27-44, and 21-32 horsepower models.

The Moline Plow Company of Moline, Illinois, bought the Universal Tractor Company of Columbus, Ohio, in 1915, in order to begin producing tractors. The Universal was a very advanced row-crop tractor for the period, even though it only had a two-cylinder engine. However, in 1918, the four-cylinder Moline Universal Model D was launched. It came with many advantages, such as low weight (3,380 pounds), high clearance (29 1/2 inches), the adaptability of horse-drawn implements, self-starter, and operating controls and levers close at hand. It also had the benefit of 98 percent of the weight on the driving wheels. None of these advantages really helped the sales. The cost was the major factor: the Fordson was about a third cheaper than the Moline D, and so sales finished in 1923.

In 1929, the Minneapolis-Moline Company of Minneapolis, Minnesota, was formed by the

The last known complete Model 15-30 Twin City from 1916. The smallest of the big Twin City tractors was expensive at $1,200 and a poor seller.

merger of the Minneapolis Steel and Machinery Company of Minneapolis, the Moline Implement Company of Moline, Illinois, and the Minneapolis Threshing Company of Hopkins, Minnesota. The new company was able to offer a full line of equipment and tractors to the farmer.

The new M-M Company had a wide range of tractors in 1930, using the Twin City name on the TC 17-28, TC 21-32, and, later, the TC 27-44 models. The Minneapolis line of tractors were the 17-30

A and B, the 27-42, and the 39-57 horsepower models, all with the famous Minneapolis cross-mounted overhead-valve four-cylinder engines. These tractor models were phased out or, like the 21-32, evolved into the FT. In 1935, the improved KTA, MTA, and FTA models were launched. The KTA was the "Kombination Tractor," meant to compete with the John Deere GP as a 3- to 4-plow tractor.

The Universal M, later called the MTA, was the successful row-crop tractor that stayed in

A Twin City 40 built in 1916. The four-cylinder overhead-valve engine has a 7 1/4-inch bore and a 9-inch stroke.

production until 1938. The Universal J Model of 1934 was the first M-M row-crop 2- to 3-plow tractor with sliding hubs on the rear axle.

In late 1936, the Z Series was launched. The Twin City name went and the M-M badges were used on the entire tractor range in the new color scheme of Prairie Gold, with red wheels. The Z used an unusual engine, with half overhead valve and half side valve. The cylinders were cast in pairs and the main bearings could be removed, with the

engine in place, through side panels. The ZTU row-crop was rated at 26.39 drawbar horsepower and 31.14 belt horsepower on gasoline fuel.

The UDLX Comfortractor, launched in 1938, gained much publicity for M-M, with its modern integral cab. But with a price tag of $2,155, it was not popular with the farmers. Only 150 were sold up to the end of production in 1941.

In World War II, M-M built many tractors for the military. The best-known was the NTX

The Moline Universal Model D was produced between 1918 and 1923. It was one of the first row-crop tractors manufactured, and could use adapted horse-drawn implements. Note the concrete inside the drive wheel for better traction.

four-by-four, using the 36-horsepower Z Series engine. A number of these were assigned to the Minnesota National Guard in 1940. A guardsman dubbed the vehicle a "Jeep" after a character in the "Popeye" cartoons. The name stuck.

Postwar models , like the R and U models, were a continuation of the prewar models. New M-M tractor models were slow to appear, due to the 1946 strikes.

The Model G, introduced in 1940, evolved into the GB in 1955. The gasoline engine

This 1918 Moline Universal Model D has a four-cylinder overhead-valve engine.

was rated at 61/68 horsepower, and the optional diesel six-cylinder was rated at 58/65 horsepower and called the GB-D. These models stayed in production until 1959. The Z became the ZB, using the 206-ci four-cylinder engine with a 3 5/8 x 5 inch bore and stroke. The U Series UB used the larger 283-ci four-cylinder M-M diesel engine. The M-M diesel tractors sold well, and the company also manufactured the Massey Ferguson 97, which was an M-M G705/6 and G707/8. Nonetheless, to survive the ever-increasing and competitive market, and to maintain their business, Minneapolis-Moline merged with the White Farm Equipment Corporation in 1963.

This 1955 Minneapolis-Moline GB diesel, a large 7,400-pound tractor, was designed for the big farms of the midwestern prairies.

The Minneapolis-Moline Twin City Universal JT row crop was manufactured from 1934 to 1937. The four-cylinder 196-ci engine featured a large oil filter and an oil-bath air cleaner mounted in front of the radiator. A five-speed transmission and a weight of only 3,450 pounds gave good performance.

This view of a 1948 Minneapolis-Moline UTC shows the offset steering that is mounted on the transmission bell housing.

Rod Flint plows at the European plowing championship with his 1938 Minneapolis-Moline ZTU row-crop. The plow is an M-M Tumblebug Reversible from the 1940s.

The Minneapolis-Moline UTC cane tractor was designed for high clearance of crops. It uses the standard overhead-valve Model U four-cylinder engine with a 4 1/2 x 5-inch bore and stroke.

CHAPTER EIGHT

Oliver, Hart-Parr, and Cockshutt

TRACTORS

The Hart-Parr Tractor Company was based in Charles City, Iowa, on the Cedar River, where it produced the first commercially viable gasoline tractor. Charles W. Hart and Charles H. Parr met at the University of Wisconsin, where both were engineering students. With the help of their tutor at the university, they built three working engines. In 1897, before they graduated, they formed the Hart-Parr Gasoline Engine Company, producing oil-cooled stationary engines for the farms. In 1900, the company moved from Madison to Charles City.

They had a fortuitous meeting with Charles Ellis, a local lawyer and banker, who gave the Hart-Parr Company a $50,000 loan. At last, the partners had enough factory space and capital to make a gasoline-engined traction engine. In

The Oliver standard 77 was manufactured from 1947 to 1954. It was sold as a three-bottom 14-inch plow tractor.

The Hart-Parr 12-24 Model E was manufactured between 1924 and 1928.

1902, the Hart-Parr Number One tractor was built, using a two-cylinder four-cycle overhead-valve horizontal engine. With a 9-inch bore and 13-inch stroke, it was rated at 30-belt horsepower. Since oil has a higher boiling point than water, oil-cooled domestic radiators were used to cool the engine. The Number One could pull up to five 14-inch plows. In 1903, 15 more machines were built, and the power was increased to 45 belt horsepower. However, it took a few years before farmers would accept the gasoline engine over the steam traction engine. Sales of the Hart-Parr machines were made more difficult by much bad publicity and fabricated stories spread by the steam traction engine companies.

In 1906, Hart-Parr Sales Manager W.H. Williams shortened the "gasoline traction engine" description in advertisements to "tractor." The Hart-Parr tractors started on gasoline fuel, but when the engine was hot, ran on kerosene, which was much cheaper. The Charles City factory became the first to manufacture tractors. This fact was advertised on the front of Hart-Parr tractors for many years, proclaiming the company as "Founders of the Tractor Industry."

In 1917, with the introduction of the Fordson tractor, Charles Ellis, the banker and business partner, wanted to produce a similar, but lighter and smaller, tractor. The big Hart-Parr weighed 6 tons. Hart and Parr were virulently against a smaller tractor. Despite their reservations, they had produced the 18-25 New Hart-Parr tractor in 1918. This modern tractor used a water-cooled two-cylinder four-cycle engine with magneto ignition and a fan-cooled radiator at the front, which was the norm. Hart and Parr did not like the new direction that the company was heading in. They sold all their stock to Ellis and left the company a few years later.

HART
PARR

HART-PARR
"30"

HART-PARR CO.
FOUNDERS OF THE
R INDUSTRY

IOWA, U.S.A

The Oliver Hart-Parr 18-28 was manufactured between 1930 and 1937. It was the standard-tread version of the row-crop 18-27. In Canada, this four-cylinder overhead-valve-engined tractor was sold as the Cockshutt Hart-Parr 18-28.

The Hart-Parr 30 Model A of 1920 was rated as a 15-30 horsepower tractor. The two-cylinder side-by-side horizontal engine has a bore of 6 1/2 inches and a stroke of 6 inches.

Charles Ellis ran the company successfully and introduced ten new models, including the four-cylinder 28-50. In 1928, due to ill health, Charles passed control to his son, Melvin.

In 1929, Melvin Ellis merged the Hart-Parr Company with Nichols & Shepard Threshing Machine Company, the American Seeding Machine Company, and the Oliver Chilled Plow Works. The new company was called the Oliver Farm Equipment Company.

The Oliver standard 77 six-cylinder diesel engine has a bore of 3.31 inches and a stroke of 3.75 inches, making a displacement of 194 ci, the same as the gasoline and LPG engines.

Joseph Oliver was head of the Oliver Chilled Plow Works, which was started by his father, James. James Oliver was born in Roxburghshire in Scotland in 1823, and moved with his parents to America in 1834. They lived at first in Geneva, on the Erie Canal, then moved west to Indiana, settling at Mishawauka. James had only one year of schooling before his father died, and he had to go to work on the riverboats. He was a hard worker and he accumulated enough money to buy a foundry in 1855. Here he set about designing a cast-iron plow that would not break. It took him many years to develop his famous chilled plow.

An Oliver Super 66, built in 1955, with live PTO and adjustable wide front axle. This is a four-cylinder gasoline engine of 144-ci displacement.

The Oliver chilled plow was designed for heavy soil. The plow was grooved with strengthening ribbing, the surface chilled with cold water when white hot to harden the plow face and give it a smooth wear-resistant surface.

When James Oliver died in 1908, his son, Joseph, became head of the very successful company. With Joseph at the helm, the company continued to flourish, and he organized the

This Oliver 88 standard has the powerful six-cylinder 231-ci gasoline engine. It has enough power to pull a four-bottom plow.

merger in 1929 to form the Oliver Farm Equipment Company.

This merger offered the new firm a full line of tractors, tillage tools, and farm implements to battle against John Deere and Company, International Harvester, and all the other competition.

In 1929, Hart-Parr had already got three sizes of tractors in production, the 12-24, 18-36, and 28-50. These models were all updated, but in 1930, the 18-27, 18-28, and 28-44 were launched with the Hart-Parr name on the radiator, with a smaller Oliver name below. All the new models were conventional tractors, using vertical engines. This series of tractors stayed in production from 1930 to 1937, despite the Great Depression. Having survived this period, tractor sales were expanding again in 1934, and Oliver set about developing their new range of tractors.

The Oliver Hart-Parr 70, with a stylized automobile design, came out in 1935 and immediately made the opposition look dated. The Oliver name was now prominent on the radiator, with a small "Hart-Parr" below. The smooth six-cylinder 201-ci engine was available in gasoline or kerosene distillate configurations on standard-tread, row-crop, high-crop, and orchard models. The unstyled Oliver 80 appeared in 1937, based on the old 18-28 four-cylinder engine tractor.

The Fleetline Series was introduced in 1937, with the Oliver 70. This was basically the same as the earlier model, but with more modern styling. The Hart-Parr name was finally dropped from the radiator in favor of the Oliver name. The 90 Standard with a four-cylinder engine was produced from 1937 to

1953, although it was fitted with the six-cylinder engine in its last year of production. The Fleetline 60 was produced from 1940 to 1948. The Standard and Fleetline Series were sold in Canada in Cockshutt colors.

The next series was the double-number series, beginning with the 99, which stayed in production from 1937 to 1957. The 99 was a heavyweight tractor of 7,500 pounds and was powered by the six-cylinder Lavona diesel engine of 302 ci. The 88, built from 1947 to 1954, had Fleetline styling and a six-cylinder 231-ci engine in gasoline or diesel versions. The 77, produced during the same period, had the gasoline or diesel six-cylinder engine of 194 ci. In the 88 and 77, large-capacity kerosene/distillate engines of 265 ci and 216 ci were used.

These models were superseded by the Super Series, built from 1954 to 1958. The new Super 55 and 66 tractors used the four-cylinder Oliver 144-ci 34-horsepower diesel or gasoline engines, with six-speed transmission. The Super 99, top of the range, used the six-cylinder 302-ci Oliver diesel engine, or the 213-ci three-cylinder two-stroke GM blower diesel engine. The Super 77 was rated as a 44-horsepower tractor with the 216-ci diesel or gas engine.

The next development for Oliver was the 100 Series in 1958, which lasted through to the takeover of the company by the White Motor Corporation of Cleveland, Ohio, in 1960. Today, the White tractor division is owned by the most-successful tractor conglomerate in the world, AGCO.

The Cockshutt name was made famous by their designs and the manufacturing of their plows.

In the late 1870s, James G. Cockshutt invented the "Sulky Plow." His plow had a unique cam for raising and lowering the plow blade. It was just what the farmers needed for the vast areas of difficult virgin land in central

A 1956 Cockshutt 35 Deluxe. It is powered by a Hercules 198-ci gasoline engine rated at 33 drawbar horsepower.

Canada. The riding plow saved time and energy compared to the walking plow.

James G. was named after his grandfather, who had emigrated to Muddy York in Ontario, Canada, from Lancashire in northern England, in 1827. The maiden name of his grandmother, Mary Cockshutt, was Nightingale, and she was sister of Florence Nightingale, known for founding the nursing profession. Florence, after working in the Crimean War and the appalling conditions in the hospitals of the nineteenth century, lived to the age of 90. James G., the grandfather, was not so lucky; he died at the young age of 34 in 1885, from tuberculosis.

James G. Cockshutt's company started in 1877, and was called the Brantford Plow Works. Then, in 1882, due to great demand, he expanded the factory with money raised by new shareholders. The new company employed 50 workers, with James G. as president and his father, Ignatius, as vice-president. The company name was changed to the Cockshutt Plow Company. Despite James G.'s early death, the Cockshutt family kept managerial control up to 1957. From the beginning of the company, the Cockshutt factory produced plows, cultivators, rollers, and planters. As the years passed, however, more and more farming products, including 12-bottom gang plows for traction engines, were manufactured.

Until World War I, the Cockshutt Company had increased the workforce to 1,500 in Brantford, Ontario. They had acquired the Adams Wagon Company, the Brantford Carriage Company, and the Frost and Wood Company, which made binders, mowers, and rakes. During World War I, Cockshutt built wagons and carriages for the military, which were shipped from Ontario to Europe.

The Cockshutt 20 was manufactured from 1952 to 1958. It initially used the Continental F-124 engine, but soon changed to the Continental F-140 engine. The engine number indicates the cubic-inch displacement.

The Cockshutt Plow Company, like other farming companies, struggled through the Depression. The high note in the early 1930s was the success of the Cockshutt "Tiller-Combine," which combined tilling and planting in one machine, saving fuel and time. In World War II, the company employed 6,000 workers, building landing-gear components and wooden fuselages for the de Havilland Mosquito bombers, and also built ambulances.

As the end of the hostilities could be seen in late 1944 and early 1945, Cockshutt and other manufacturers began designing and testing new products.

The Cockshutt Company had marketed Hart-Parr tractors in Canada from 1924 to 1928, then Allis-Chalmers, with Cockshutt nameplates, from 1928 to 1934. This was followed by a long agreement with Oliver Hart-Parr in 1934 to market their tractors, but in Cockshutt colors.

The standard-type Oliver tractors, like the 80, came with a cast-iron radiator surround with the Cockshutt name in relief. Some early models, until 1938, also included the Hart-Parr name below the Cockshutt name. The modern-looking streamlined Oliver tractors, built at Charles City, Iowa, were known as the Fleetline Series. These were also built as Cockshutts in 1937 with the same Oliver body hood panels, but with the Cockshutt name painted down the center of the radiator grill. These models were painted red with cream- or off-white-colored wheels and radiator grill. The prewar colors were carried over to the new range of postwar Cockshutt tractors, designed and built in Brantford, Ontario, Canada.

A 1958 Cockshutt 20 Deluxe. Its Continental four-cylinder gasoline engine produced 28 horsepower in this 4,500-pound lightweight tractor.

The new range of tractors was similar in design and shape to the prewar Oliver Fleetline tractors, but with new and useful improvements. Like other tractor manufacturers, there were none of the side engine covers that had become popular in the late 1930s. These had put costs up, and many farmers took them off anyway. Quick access to the engine was more important than keeping the engine clean.

The first tractor offered was the Cockshutt 30 in 1946, using the Buda four-cylinder valve-in-head 153-ci engine. Initially, two versions were offered, gasoline and distillate, then later diesel and liquefied petroleum gas models. A four-speed transmission was standard with an option of underdrive, giving eight forward and two reverse gears. The most important feature of the Cockshutt 30 was the pioneering of live PTO, a first for a tractor, which all the other tractor manufacturers followed.

The successful Cockshutt 30 was in production from 1946 to 1956. It was also marketed as the CO-OP E3 and the Gamble Farmcrest 30. In

1949, the Cockshutt 40 tractor was built, using the six-cylinder Buda engine of 230 ci with a six-speed gearbox. This tractor was also sold as the CO-OP E4. Production of the 40 lasted until the end of 1957.

In 1952, the Cockshutt 20 tractor, designed for small farms and market gardens, was produced. It used gasoline and distillate four-cylinder Continental F engines of, initially, 124 ci and, later, 140 ci. The 20 was also marketed as the CO-OP E2.

In 1953, the biggest Cockshutt tractor in this series arrived as the 50 and D50, using the Buda six-cylinder 273-ci engine in gasoline or diesel form. This was also marketed as the CO-OP E5.

In the new Cockshutt 40D4 tractor of 1954, only the Perkins four-cylinder diesel was offered. Cockshutt had been forced to sever its good working relationship with Buda after Allis-Chalmers took over the well-known engine builders.

In 1956, the type 30 was changed to the type 35, with the fitting of the Hercules 198-ci four-cylinder engine.

In 1958, the new 500 Series, with the body designed by Raymond Loewy, was produced and continued until 1962. This series of Cockshutts was offered with a wide variety of engines, all with six-speed transmissions, live PTO, and hydraulics.

The 550 used the four-cylinder 198-ci Hercules engine. The 560 used the Perkins of Great Britain 269.5-ci diesel engine. The 570 used the six-cylinder 298-ci Hercules engine.

The beginning of the end of the Cockshutt Company was during the years of 1955 to 1957, with a worldwide overproduction of tractors. In 1957, the Cockshutt Plow Company was taken over by the English Transcontinental Company. Canadian press reports of the new company being an "asset stripper" proved to be a correct description. In 1961, part of the factory in Brantford, and the rights to the agricultural equipment, were sold to White, and the rest of the factory was demolished. A sad end to a world-famous company.

Clubs and Newsletters

These clubs are run by enthusiasts specializing in individual brands of vintage farm tractors. They offer an abundance of information, as well as help in authentic restorations and in sourcing parts. The following is an up-to-date list at the time of publication.

Antique Power, Editor Patrick Ertel, P.O. Box 838, Yellow Springs, OH 45387.

Green Magazine, Editor Richard Hain, R.R.1, Bee, NE 68314. (John Deere)

IH Collectors, R.R. 2, Box 286, Winimac, IN 46996. (International Harvester)

M-M Corresponder, Editor Roger Mohr, Rt. 1, Box 153, Vail, IA 51465. (Minneapolis-Moline)

9N-2N-8N Newsletter, Editor G.W. Rinaldi, P.O. Box 235, Chelsea, VT 05038-0235. (Ford)

Old Abe News, Editor David T. Erb, Rt. 2, Box 2427, Vinton, OH 45686. (Case)

J.I. Case Heritage Foundation, Box 5128, Bella Vista, AR 72714-0128.

Old Allis News, Editor Nan Jones, 10925 Love Road, Belleview, MI 49021. (Allis-Chalmers)

Oliver Collector's News, Editor Dennis Gerszewski, Rt. 1, Manvel, ND 58256-0044. (Oliver)

Prairie Gold Rush, Editor R. Baumgartner, Rt. 1, Walnut, IL 61376. (Minneapolis-Moline)

Red Power, Editor Daryl Miller, Box 277, Battle Creek, IA 51006. (International Harvester)

Wild Harvest, Editor Keith Oltrogge, 1010 S. Powell, Box 529, Denver, IA 50622. (Massey-Harris-Ferguson)

Annual Directory of Tractor, Threshing and Steam Shows, Stemgas Publishing Company, P.O. Box 328, Lancaster, PA 17603.

INDEX